TOP 10 MOMENTS IN GYMNASTICS

BY NATHAN SOMMER

Minneapolis, Minnesota

Credits

Cover and title page, © Aflo Co. Ltd./Alamy Stock Photo and © Sportlibrary/Adobe Stock and © vitaliy_melnik/Adobe Stock; 4, © Juice Dash/Shutterstock and © nycshooter/iStock and © FG Trade/iStock and © kali9/iStock and © T–kin/iStock and © marieclaudelemay/iStock and © Jadon/Adobe Stock and © Yuri Arcurs/Adobe Stock and © Iuliia/Adobe Stock and © caluian/Adobe Stock and © Pavlovski Israel/Adobe Stock and © Sportpoint/Adobe Stock and © Petr Joura/Adobe Stock and © samards/Adobe Stock and © Microgen/Adobe Stock and © Artur Didyk/Adobe Stock and © Gecko Studio/Adobe Stock and © Victoria Viar Pro/Adobe Stock and © Alex/Adobe Stock and © Yolanda Garcia Foto/Adobe Stock and © Iakov Filimonov/Adobe Stock and © Tatiana Morozova/Adobe Stock and © master1305/Adobe Stock and © Sportlibrary/Adobe Stock and © Jax__Sorax/Adobe Stock and © Chris Van Lennep/Adobe Stock and © Uzfoto/Adobe Stock and © samards/Adobe Stock; 5, © Suzanne Vlamis/Associated Press; 6, © Don Morley/Getty Images; 7, © Colorsport/Shutterstock; 8, © Peter Read Miller/Getty Images; 8–9, © Gregory Bull/Associated Press; 10, © Susan Ragan/Associated Press; 11, © Mike Powell/Getty Images; 12, © Tim Clayton /Getty Images; 13, © The Asahi Shimbun/Getty Images; 14, © Fabrice Coffrini/Getty Images; 14–15, © Tim Clayton /Getty Images; 16–17, © Bob Thomas/Getty Images; 17, © David Madison/Getty Images; 18, © Leo Mason/Popperfoto/Getty Images; 19, © Ernie Mastroianni/ Alamy Stock Photo; 20, © Popperfoto/Getty Images; 21, © The Asahi Shimbun/Getty Images; 22TR, © Doug Pensinger/Getty Images; 22ML, © Yoshikazu Tsuno/Getty Images; 22BR, © Ezra Shaw/Getty Images; 23BR, © Adil Yusifov/Adobe Stock

Bearport Publishing Company Product Development Team

Publisher: Jen Jenson; Director of Product Development: Spencer Brinker; Editorial Director: Allison Juda; Editor: Cole Nelson; Editor: Tiana Tran; Production Editor: Naomi Reich; Art Director: Kim Jones; Designer: Kayla Eggert; Designer: Steve Scheluchin; Production Specialist: Owen Hamlin

Statement on Usage of Generative Artificial Intelligence

Bearport Publishing remains committed to publishing high-quality nonfiction books. Therefore, we restrict the use of generative AI to ensure accuracy of all text and visual components pertaining to a book's subject. See BearportPublishing.com for details.

Library of Congress Cataloging-in-Publication Data is available at www.loc.gov or upon request from the publisher.

ISBN: 979-8-89577-064-1 (hardcover)
ISBN: 979-8-89577-511-0 (paperback)
ISBN: 979-8-89577-181-5 (ebook)

Copyright © 2026 Bearport Publishing Company. All rights reserved. No part of this publication may be reproduced in whole or in part, stored in any retrieval system, or transmitted in any form or by any means, electronic, mechanical, photocopying, recording, or otherwise, without written permission from the publisher. Bearport Publishing is a division of FlutterBee Education Group.

For more information, write to Bearport Publishing, 3500 American Blvd W, Suite 150, Bloomington, MN 55431.

CONTENTS

A Long History. 4

#10 The First Perfect 10. 5

#9 Fujimoto Fights On 6

#8 Douglas Sees Double 8

#7 Vault for Gold. 10

#6 Uchimura Repeats History. 12

#5 An Olympic Record 13

#4 Biles Breaks Out 14

#3 Team USA's Upset 16

#2 A Picture-Perfect Landing 18

#1 The Korbut Flip .20

Even More Extreme Gymnastics Moments 22

Glossary. 23

Index 24

Read More. 24

Learn More Online 24

About the Author 24

A LONG HISTORY

Artistic gymnastics dates back thousands of years to ancient Greece. But it wasn't until the early 1800s that *artistic gymnastics* became an actual term. Over time, gymnastics has become one of the most-watched Olympic events.

WHAT ARE THE TOP 10 MOMENTS IN OLYMPIC GYMNASTICS?

Read on to decide for yourself. . . .

#10 THE FIRST PERFECT 10

July 18, 1976 • Montreal Forum • Montreal, Quebec

Many thought a **perfect 10** at the Olympics was impossible. But in 1976, Romania's Nadia Comăneci made it happen. Her faultless performance on the **uneven bars** made her the first to receive this honor. During the competition, Comăneci went on to gain six more perfect scores. This earned her three gold medals!

Comăneci was only 14 years old during the 1976 Olympics.

At the time, the scoreboards weren't even designed to show a score of 10.

In 2006, gymnastic rules changed. A 10 was no longer a perfect score.

#9 FUJIMOTO FIGHTS ON

July 20, 1976 • Montreal Forum • Montreal, Quebec

Japan's Fujimoto Shun hurt his kneecap at the 1976 Olympics. However, he kept the injury hidden from his team and went on to compete. To end his **rings** routine, Shun needed to drop from 8 feet (2 m) above the ground and stick a landing . . . on his broken knee! His 9.7 score helped Japan win the gold.

From 1960–1976, the Japanese men's team won five straight gold medals.

The Japanese men's team in 1976

Shun received a 9.5 score for his **pommel horse** routine, also done while injured.

Shun waited to reveal his injury until after his rings performance.

The 9.7 score was a personal best for Shun.

After 1976, Japan did not win gold again until 2004.

#8 DOUGLAS SEES DOUBLE

August 2, 2012 ▪ The O2 Arena ▪ London, England

Team USA's Gabby Douglas dominated the 2012 Olympics. She was the only U.S. gymnast to compete in every event during the team finals, helping earn the team gold. Douglas also won gold in the individual **all-around** event. This made her the first American ever to win gold medals in both the team and individual all-around events.

The 2012 U.S. team was nicknamed the Fierce Five.

Douglas was the first Black American to win individual all-around gold.

Douglas helped the U.S. team win gold again in the 2016 Olympics.

The gold-medal win was the first for team USA since 1996.

#7 VAULT FOR GOLD

July 23, 1996 • Georgia Dome • Atlanta, Georgia

At the 1996 Olympics, the U.S. team had a small lead during the all-around finals. But then, during Kerri Strug's first **vault**, she sprained her ankle. The team needed her to perform well on her next vault for the win. Strug vaulted again and stuck the landing! Her 9.712 score earned the team its gold medal.

Strug had to be carried to the podium to celebrate the U.S. victory.

Strug being carried by coach Béla Károlyi

The 1996 U.S. team was nicknamed the Magnificent Seven.

The U.S. women's team had never won team gold before the 1996 Olympics.

After her final vault, Strug couldn't compete for the rest of the Olympics.

#6 UCHIMURA REPEATS HISTORY

August 10, 2016 • HSBC Arena • Rio de Janeiro, Brazil

Japan's Kōhei Uchimura was on a roll going into the 2012 Olympics. He continued to dominate, winning gold in the individual all-around—and then did it again in 2016! With his incredible **high bar** routine, he became the first male gymnast in 44 years to win back-to-back individual gold medals.

In 2016, Uchimura beat Ukraine's Oleg Verniaiev by only 0.099 points.

Uchimura is considered by many to be the greatest male gymnast of all time.

Uchimura also won gold in the team competition at the 2016 Olympics.

#5 AN OLYMPIC RECORD

October 23, 1964 ▪ Tokyo Metropolitan Gymnasium ▪ Tokyo, Japan

In 1964, Russia's Larisa Latynina competed in her third-straight Olympics. She won gold in the team all-around and **floor exercise** events. She also received two silver and two bronze medals. Latynina finished her career with a total of 18 Olympic medals. At the time, this was the most of any athlete in history. Latynina's record stood unbroken for 48 years.

From 1956–1964, Latynina won 14 individual medals and 4 team medals.

Latynina won team gold at every Olympics she competed in.

Out of Latynina's 18 medals, 9 were gold.

13

#4 BILES BREAKS OUT

August 9, 2016 ▪ HSBC Arena ▪ Rio de Janeiro, Brazil

Team USA's Simone Biles made her mark at the 2016 Olympics. First, Biles won team gold. Then, she wowed with first place finishes in the vault, floor exercise, and individual all-around events. Biles became the first American gymnast to win four gold medals at one Olympics. It set off a winning streak that continued for years to come!

Biles was Team USA's **flag bearer** for the closing ceremonies of the Rio Olympics.

Biles was the first female gymnast to win four gold medals at one Olympics since 1984.

At the 2016 Olympics, Biles also won bronze for the **balance beam**.

Biles went on to win three more gold medals at the 2024 Olympics.

Team USA Gymnastics won a total of nine medals in 2016. This is the most in team history.

15

#3 TEAM USA'S UPSET

July 31, 1984 ▪ Pauley Pavilion ▪ Los Angeles, California

China was favored to win the men's team competition at the 1984 Olympics. Instead, they were defeated by the United States! Team USA's Mitch Gaylord scored a perfect 10 on the rings. Then, his teammate Bart Conner scored another 10 on the parallel bars. Each outstanding routine helped Team USA ultimately defeat China by only 0.6 points!

The shocking upset was the first and only U.S. gold medal in men's team gymnastics.

The 1984 men's gymnastics team is considered one of the greatest in U.S. gymnastics history.

Conner performing on the parallel bars

Conner also won gold in the individual parallel bars at this Olympics.

Team USA had not won any medals in the team all-around competition since 1932.

#2 A PICTURE-PERFECT LANDING

August 3, 1984 ▪ Pauley Pavilion ▪ Los Angeles, California

The women's individual all-around competition at the 1984 Olympics came down to a single vault. Team USA's Mary Lou Retton needed a perfect 10 to beat Romania's Ecaterina Szabo. Retton soared in the air, twisting over the vault. Then, she stuck the landing of a lifetime! Retton received a perfect 10. She defeated Szabo by only 0.05 points.

Retton became the first female American gymnast to win individual all-around gold.

During the floor exercise, Retton also received a perfect 10.

Szabo led Retton by 0.15 points with 2 events left in the competition.

Retton had knee surgery six weeks before the 1984 games.

19

#1 THE KORBUT FLIP

September 1, 1972 ▪ Olympic Hall ▪ Munich, Germany

Belarus's Olga Korbut changed gymnastics forever at the 1972 Games. Korbut swung backward on the uneven bars, completing a backflip from a handstand. Then, she successfully grabbed the bar! Korbut was the first gymnast to try this daring backflip in an international competition. Many credit her with turning gymnastics into the acrobatic sport it is today.

Korbut won three gold medals at the 1972 Olympics.

Korbut backflipping on the balance beam

Korbut is also the first Olympian to do a backward somersault on the balance beam.

This iconic move became known as the Korbut Flip.

Judges were booed after Korbut received her score of 9.8. People thought she deserved a perfect 10.

EVEN MORE EXTREME GYMNASTICS MOMENTS

Gymnastics have been a part of every Summer Olympics since the start of modern Olympics in 1896. Here are some other extreme moments from the sport's history.

XIAOSHUANG'S NARROW VICTORY
At the 1996 games, China's Li Xiaoshuang defeated Russia's Alexei Nemov by one of the smallest **margins** in Olympics history. While Nemo scored 9.7, Xiaoshung earned 9.787 points.

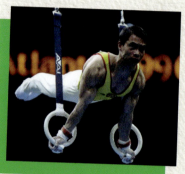

KHORKINA WINS GOLD
During the 1996 Olympics, Russia's Svetlana Khorkina finished in 15th place in the individual all-around after falling on the uneven bars. She got another chance at the uneven bars final and won gold!

MARONEY'S VAULT
American McKayla Maroney landed a near-perfect vault during the 2012 Olympics. She scored 16.233 points. This is the highest scoring vault ever in women's gymnastics!

22

GLOSSARY

all-around an event that determines the best overall individual and team gymnasts based on the combined score of their performances in different events

balance beam an event in which a flat, rectangular beam is used in women's gymnastics

flag bearer the athlete chosen to carry their country's flag at the opening or closing ceremony of the Olympics

floor exercise an event in which gymnasts compete on a floor mat without using any equipment

high bar an event in which male gymnasts perform on a horizontal bar 9.2 ft. (2.8 m) above the ground

margins the amount of points by which events are won

perfect 10 until 2006, the top possible score an olympic gymnast could receive

pommel horse an event in which male gymnasts perform on a large rectangular base with handles

rings an event in which male gymnasts perform on two rings suspended above the ground by straps

uneven bars an event in which female gymnasts perform on long bars that are positioned at different heights

vault an event in which gymnasts run, jump, and launch themselves over a vaulting table at the end of a runway

INDEX

bronze 13, 15
finals 8, 10, 22
gold 5-18, 20, 22
history 4, 12-13, 15, 22
individual 8-9, 12-14, 16, 18, 22
injury 6-7
landing 6, 10, 18, 22
perfect 10 5, 16, 18-19, 21
record 13
routine 6-7, 12, 16
silver 13
team 6, 8-18

READ MORE

McDougall, Chrös. *Olympic Gymnastics (Olympic Sports).* Minneapolis: ABDO Publishing, 2025.

Scheffer, Janie. *Best Gymnastics Teams (All-Access Gymnastics).* Minneapolis: Lerner Publications, 2024.

LEARN MORE ONLINE

1. Go to **FactSurfer.com** or scan the QR code below.
2. Enter "**10 Gymnastics Moments**" into the search box.
3. Click on the cover of this book to see a list of websites.

ABOUT THE AUTHOR

Nathan Sommer graduated from the University of Minnesota with degrees in journalism and political science. He lives in Minneapolis, Minnesota, and enjoys camping, hiking, and writing in his free time.